The Healing Tree
a book of poetry, prose, meditations & affirmations

Dr. Tytianna Nikia Maria Ringstaff

This book is in memory of and dedicated to my daughter, Nadia Michelle Robinson (born an angel on May 19, 2005)

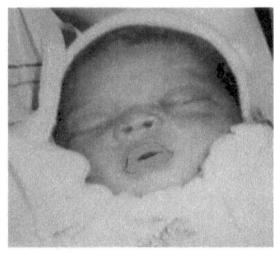

Honey Tree Publishing
www.honeytreepublishingus.com

All rights reserved under Honey Tree Publishing. No part of this book can be reproduced or transmitted in any form or by any means, electronic or mechanical, including photocopying, recording, or by any information storage and retrieval system, without permission in writing from the Publisher. Published in the United States by Honey Tree Publishing, Kentucky.

Library of Congress Cataloging-in-Publication Data
Ringstaff, Dr. Tytianna Nikia Maria, 1987-
The healing tree: a book of poetry, prose, meditations
& affirmations.
1. Poetry. 2. Nonfiction. 3. Autobiography. 4. Storytelling.

I. Ringstaff, Dr. Tytianna Nikia Maria., ill. II. Title.

ISBN-10: 0-692-94178-9/ ISBN-13: 978-0-692-94178-2/
Paperback-2017

Book designed by Dr. Tytianna Nikia Maria Ringstaff

Manufactured in the United States of America

Table of Contents

When **R a i n** Clouds **G a t h e r**　　　　*SPRING*

Part One: H o p e

that day　　　　　　　　4

Two Years Later　　　　7

Night-watcher　　　　　9

Fifth Birthday　　　　　10

Storm Clouds Gather　　11

A **J a r** of **C a n e**　　　　　　*SUMMER*

Part One: D e e p Tree **R o o t s**

the journey　　　　　　16

tomorrow　　　　　　　22

Eve's Cosmogram　　　　23

Root Doctor　　　　　　26

Drum Circle　　　　　　30

Fertile Ground　　　　　33

Wombman　　　　　　　35

Part Two: Sweet **R i v e r s** Run **S t i l l**

Big Momma's Hands　　　38

A Mother's Child　　　　39

One Hand at a Time　　　40

Proverbs 4:23　　　　　　43

One Lesson to the Next	46
a call on monday morning	49

Beyond the Sycamores — *AUTUMN*

Part One: *C a n d l e l i t* **Lanterns**

In the Meantime	53
Candlelight	55
Leaving Him	57
Magic	58
Remembering July	59
Belong to Me	60
Sacred	61
i will	63

Part Two: *It Don't S h i n e Like It Used To*

welfare ballad	65
mademoiselle ebony	67
Bystanders	68
the jungle	69
Mama Works	71
She's Baby Mines	73
Inside Home Pt. 1	75
sirens	79
A Mother's Tears	81

Inside Home Pt. 2   84

Happily Ever After   88

An Intricate T a p e s t r y   *WINTER*

Part One: *With G O D*

A Daughter's Prayer   94

A 101 Year Legacy   95

Sap and Leaves   98

SHE: A ballad for sistah   100

Behind my Skin   103

Just Become   105

Healing   106

Manifesting   108

About the Author   109

Preface

If it weren't for God and the child that he allowed me to carry and birth, I would not be the woman that I am today. I started writing this book when I was 18 years old. Over the past 12-years, I have prayed over the words, dreams, and plans that this book encases. I have endured many seasons as I birthed and buried my first child before graduating from high school with a full academic scholarship, studied and traveled internationally, earned several college degrees, laid my father to rest, launched a book publishing company, married my dream husband, taught children all over the world, completed a PhD, and continue to follow God's Plan for my life.

It has not been an easy road but God kept me and still keeps me. I would like to give all praise to God who is the Creator and my strength. Through the struggles and victories, I have been blessed by many people over the years. Many have been present in my life for an extended period of time, while others, only for a season. And during that time, an impact was made. Thank you for your comforting words, hugs, stories, and love.

My dearest reader, as an artist, storyteller, writer, poet/spoken-word artist, and teacher, my prayer is to always share my story as a testimony to bless the people around me. I hope you are encouraged to also tell your story as you manifest your passion and purpose to fulfill your innermost potential, hopes and aspirations. Thank you

Peacefully,

Tytianna

Louisville, Kentucky, August 22, 2017

When Rain Clouds Gather

SPRING

PART ONE

H o p e

*He told me to
keep hope
so, I laid my body down
without sound*

that day
___

prayers
seep from my lips
my womb is
sinking.

      asphyxiate
bottomless and raw.
excretion of soul
scream shudder
      scream
quiet.

motions are paused slowly
understood interlock of
memory palms a
lukewarm prayer.

      "what God?"

demons flew from his nose
onto my lap. each one,
dancing with bells. ruby
tender to heart dissipation.
black oil lines, streaking
melon-flushed cheeks.

they know

knees collapse
neck extends
fingers stiffen
torso curves body
jerks tongue
bleeds mouth
gaps open
voice is voiceless

the child has
died as
i
caress the uterus womb
 it
shifted
and fell
before i
could
catch
it

"mama loves her baby girl," i told her.

she remained still. i held
that child
               alone

          mode

the room grew cold
     as her skin

the room darkened as
    her skin

fingers web interlaced a natural cradle only
a mother can build   i grip her firmly and
close. breasts full with birth milk sore and
chocked i brush my cheek against hers

"why not me Lord?"

hoping for an answer. searching
for an answer

breathing

breathing

Two Years Later
---

too many tears times the son who left my
arms empty equals too much.

but you were a girl before the bright child a
brand new sparkle.

this life was in me
and, i can only
feel it.
dies with the last one hung

last in
the family on oliver
now.

shoveled upon her tiny features
and pink fabric bought

last bit of what i got
but she all i got and
she all i had.

    until the son twinned the womb
    shown itself
    two times

was then i held my limbs
stretched out open

the last time i cried
arms were empty arms
were reaching finger
bones reaching deep
inside that shedding tree bark

now i know where to find her under
her brother's arm
right under your brother

it's been two years since
my womb
emptied into my arms

and you can't
tell me i
don't feel
a
thang

Night-watcher

This night is a wicked one splitting mirrors in rust-
covered spaces rolling up sleeves are warped scars
are crayon marks on black boards pull from my
scalp cords hair cords plucked from my scalp.

Hold them open wide these dark holes in my face
lines the pit of my joints be the last thing on earth to
smell the coming of rain from someone's fenced-in
synergy be making pine needles stab at my womb-
baby. A circle in birthing fluid and vomit and
thunder can't have you licking the raw, thick-rope
blood veins down my thighs.

Brown love baby butter retreats
at sunrise 4:25am across the sky
clock on my watch
are bulging eyes and organs
that await
my next moon cry.

Fifth Birthday

Soul and spirit when I pray to
God and baby how I wish she
can hear it. They
can hear it
      thundering
I pray this heavy burden is taken from me
never felt this but I need more
to fill the void
      I need your strength
some days when the town is
loud and angry
and smoke blindly rises from each driving gutter
I want you to save me. This time
      just to know you
are able.

People are in hurries
for babies for
maybe's. Breaks this
tired heart
of mine a cradled lullaby neatly
wrapped.

Ask you to forgive me
      this child was mine
      this child
      is mine
engulfed inside my arms
    the mind of a mother - stolen

Storm Clouds Gather

storm clouds gather here colorless
rib-rage
translucent fist-fire
muddled mouth curses are verses

    he is the shadow my papa warned me about

ears shut heart
open

he wants all of me to
keep for good

    i dont believe him.

soul & legs are full & open

they say when death rests on your face no
soul can change its course
thats all that is needed
& matters

    i must carve time out of my schedule
to paint on my face, now.

rearrange contours meant for permanence
disheveled crooked dislocated my place
is not here any more i am a building

tower in a quiet city vision blur eye
socket closed salt crimson stain this love
tastes bitter

      everything will be okay girl with pink
lipstick tells me through the mirror.

          she cant feel the burn in my
skin   pine needles in my spine
    she cant feel how the earth
        turns differently for me
under my feet
        her world is not of my own

the pain is thundersome
cumbersome under a shutter-sun
that lifts from folds cracks
blinds
until the day is done

there is a bruise for each mood a
shade-shame kind of pain
to pull from
     so
i cure-remedy out the dresser drawer dab
sting of whiskey from the low-shelf diner
watch the moon crash silence black & blue

this is a love i cant nip
away at no how
but i am getting there

one day

we will
all get
there

A Jar of Cane

SUMMER

PART ONE

Deep Tree Roots

when she
took
her last breath

her children planted
a tree nearby

it was a different summer
for them

the journey

---

eve's ale a crop born from
sun-soil plant in my roots
harvest for black land mother i
named you justice love

branched in my heart
freedom vined in my
soul

      they took me & all three

under a thousand suns to a foreign one
chain metal coffle my limbs wooden
gasp cart whip order keeper

iron muzzle trap noise song
chained christened
shaved branded   liquid-
fire-melt near
rib-heart cage

      this journey will be long

five slaves per three tons

despite the ship days &
months floating on a
seafloor of tears one on top
of the other one stop
after the other

packed inside disease
swollen belly
deliverance new
promise to the world
once celebrated now
cursed by legality
hearsay

i cry until the land is blurry-blind you
throw overboard the weak & sick
from urine vomit defecation hemorrhaging womb

sweltering sun organ a
distant moon
throatcloggedfume
scream vibrations echo

      imprisonment
                  can displace
you
                          from
         the
     inside   *out*
                              you know

profiteer this voyage from
a barracoon fort by way
of sky water port elmina
bunce goree-
&

           anywhere else
       they see fit
for manchildslave

thorn cotton pod flower
sugar husk cane stalk
rice swamp tobacco
seed

             rum & cash
            wine & crop

await me

quarantine salt pork horsebean
black eye pea eight-ounce extract
    from sea
    push starch protein
               down throat choke
    speculum force-feed
    device for a beast

fattened for highest bidder
in seconds wealth power
is of the essence

      my home is far away from here

    we are growing close

cargo release jump
overboard
swim-drown

    others fly back

    return to
    mother horn
       father drum

  descendants will be soon & thereafter born
  there will be
  12 million slaves & a negra child for each one
  ocean tears run deep
  lost somewhere between
  heaven
    &
  home

night-years behind & ahead of me

  what it be like
    on the other side
    of the salt-sea
      glittering stones

stand me up
spread me wide
pinch my skin
pull out my hair
stretch open my mouth

  good breed

   i'll take this one

     that one won't do

niggar
wench
brute
heathen

savage

no one hears
the cries of
a, man-made slave
    do
they?

        i come from
        epic reflection
        in a three tier direction
    substantial baggage
        is excessive

    rest assured   this
covenant   will be
remembered   for some
time

i will recover & return to you
this place i call home look
back for it
stretch for it
        please
    recall
who i am

    i call your name
        in honor
        in sorrow
        in light
        in birth
        in chains

in liberation

         i call your name
for   wisdom
             heart
     & words

       in time,
this story
will be told

       branched from my soul

tomorrow

---

en de sunhigh daybruk

maamy hol' um milk know'mo
git summuch ov dem clots
down en um spine. chil sissy
outdo' dey urruh kin 'long'um
ain' nebbuh yeye sky cotton lukkuh dem b'fo.'

maamy gone'way de chil sissy sump'time 'go
sump'n bout le sucre d'eau, cornmeal in de cu'board
but knows fuh true. aint bin tuh cya' 'nuf load luk
sammy, rayfield en sins aint bin much too much tuh
carry. git too many ov mo'wn tuh carry

en de mawnin daybruk.

Eve's Cosmogram

silhouette physics dance upon the
upheaval goopher dust treading
footsteps, lost and finding
white shadows
engulf the darkness
seeping through
woods under a
golden moon light
gentle clicking.
bottled pressure found sacred
with honey pinch of cotton
petal sage rolled in devils
shoestring single hair strand
all found dangling messaging:

      gwine leh dey spirit en
      wen leddown muh bodee

      both souls are lifted
      by the arm tree

emerald oil leaking
from each body
hovering like
pigeons on a
mission connecting
with ivy
root sap grasping

      that's why they pace themselves
      out of
time.

one soul,
two ribbed streaks grazing the leaves

dey en de vines

the atlantic slave watch understands angry and
lonely tones. bodies hang, swaying; knocking in
sycamore leaves, willowed threads and t
windows- shudders flap as the bodies enter
upper torso cut though soot-warn pants and
skirts are there.

we all
know, but too
soon, erase
the sketch.

    chil, git out der en close um shudduhs

won't die.
circular face clocks draped around
asthmatic lungs death scroll innards
come in blue ink scented with rainwater.
each body, pregnant with sorrow under the stars
a deep vibrating moan knock violently on doors
glowing from burning kerosene this midnight
time

and

    they
    escape.

as fingerprints intertwine
and lock

they stride

brushing passed the graves of daughters,
mothers brothers sons husbands and wives
to become ancestors painted on timber

the wind knocks the clumsy bodies
together,   clinging
      to
each other. and

      their
names are chosen to stay

      to whistle
in nearby storms.

to live again
once more

Root Doctor

Tajah was a healer of sorts a
spiritualist of kinfolk gathering where
flies linger and swarm an encircled
space on someone's porch
sacred in her conjure

> *to bring me here*
> *keep me here*

plant seed flood earth and soil.
Gather together and collect the
herb. To listen closely,

> *your*
> *time has come*

> *your*
> *time*
> *is*
> *near*

broke open cane-crystal shell a dash
of sea salt from her cupboard one
garlic clove on top-stove all while
doing so hands mix medicinal
storm stew
cut open melon
meat flesh dig it
out
remedy relieve restore reverberate
to sizzle its seed to free its fumes to
fragments elements compounds particles

& stretch open its lungs
she called out a name some
name
& put inside the bowl
some thing. Blessed
with
myrrh aloes and cassia bark
baptismal waters & she
prayed on the ground
of a holy place

a type of folktale told
for centuries on end
a type of folktale told
for centuries on end

but this tale was real and
breathing
and had flesh

roll on, tumble and fly but don't
forget to remember me roll on,
tumble and fly but don't forget
to remember me roll on, tumble
and fly but don't forget to
remember me roll on, tumble
and fly
but don't
forget a
draft is
predicted
& on its
way I can
feel how
the rain
is

pouring
it glides
through
me like
hormonal
everglade
s face has
seen this
creation
before
past born
& dead
past life
& breath.

I,
too, am passing
  by & by

a type of folktale told
for centuries on end
a type of folktale told
for centuries on end

but this tale was real &
breathing
& had flesh

roll on, tumble and fly but don't
forget to remember me roll on,
tumble and fly
but don't forget

Everlasting Father
Soul lifter
Meditator

Messiah
King of Kings
I AM
Living Water
The Almighty
The Way, The Truth & the Light Spirit Guider
Spirit Guider
 Spirit
  guide her

a type of folktale told
for centuries on end
but this tale was real
& breathing
& had flesh

roll on, tumble and fly but don't
forget to remember me roll on,
tumble and fly but don't forget
to remember me roll on, tumble
and fly but don't forget to
remember me
roll on, tumble and fly

but don't
forget

Inspired by survivors of heart disease

Drum Circle

*there is but one single drum
that we exist in a
cosmology of
vibrations*

eloquent spoken her heart is heavy
and forgiving for this disease wont
take her she must tell children but
herself first victimless to the hospital
i declare war against any animosity
the monstrosity that denies my will to breathe

breathe

something that is taken for granted
until words behind the phone or
letters behind the note
or expression that says you wont
        live long
you wont
        stand strong
you denied me three times told
me to calm down
its nothing

        out of control
        out of my control

        you tell me

change is time delicate
and eternal some
things never leave
change and time
are two of those things

i will not wear the letters of my heart
for you to sing and cry for mock the
ringing phones the doctor bills
the sleepless nights

i must put on my warrior face and
smile the tears away swallow all the
words that i want to say all the doubt
pain uncertainty behind this race

stand up for myself stand
up for yourself you are a
mother
daughter sister friend lover you are a woman you
are everything that this earth has put into you and
dont you ever forget that

speak out and live your life to its
highest purpose tell your story two and
three times over
until they remember until every drop of pain that
you felt on this journey brings your heart into their
home

drum is speaking a
pulsating chamber
that I call my own

      i am a survivor

my reflection stares back at me in
the wide vanity mirror
post its photos
cards
       all greet me
remind me that it aint
over
when they say it is so
it aint so until
 it is so

God has his hands on my life this hurdle will be
one in which i jump not for me but for my
children for my descendants

this race aint won until i give all that is left in me
until my energy is all that is left in me and with
all of the apprehension celebrations
disappointments urgencies the circumstances
that name my heart do not own me

i do not wear this disease as a labeled
identity and designated litany this disease
does not define me i am the epitome of
strength
                        and i have a life to live

Fertile Ground

in three days time
baby belly will be full for nine

it was a blood moon when the
waves came crashing in beckoning
to me to feel the womb waters
gravity pull and let flow naturally

fourth day past marks the genesis
of the canal path   from seed to
conception implanting into soil
thickening embedding arms cloak
around us completed on day seven
for the coming of four seasons and
an arrival spoken into existence

prepare a pail of lukewarm lavender for
this natural organic human connection
wrap hair feet hands modestly insulate
body heat the space between womb and
world remedy the recipe roots pressure
packed in mason jars
stinging nettle
red raspberry red
clover
strawberry leaves
ceylon cinnamon
lemon grass

burn wand sage for protection
pray meditate fast cleanse the
body is a garden the spirit is

a temple sow receive to
manifest, love, exhale
inhale with womb child baby
is with us baby needs us
we need you

the ground is fruitful be
grounded the roots are
plentiful be rooted earth
garden is overflowing rhythm
vibrations all inside me womb
and garden soil and uterus
both connected
and two of the same

it took many years but the roots
were fertile all along grown at the
healing home centered and
focused balanced and open
with the spirit world

now, come into own come
into my own come into
your own and let seed let
flow let grow let breathe
into the world sound and
light drum and heart

all is well
all is well

Wombman

Live and become
cosmic conception water
womb
breathe life uterus
aesthetic
now liberation

let seed let
flow let
grow let
born let
learn let
teach let
forgive let
lead let
stand let
love let
speak
breathe life

Earth mama Birth
survivor Storm
gatherer
Womb giver
Rain maker Light
goddess
Wave turner
Root doctor Moon
gripper
Sun healer Manifest
Maat Ancestor

child breathe life let
speak let love let
stand let lead let
forgive let teach let
learn let born let
grow let flow let
seed

let breathe let
breathe

PART TWO

Sweet *R i v e r s* Run *S t i l l*

that child holds cane-sweet corn husk
under her baby belly wide and
swollen
as she high-steps through town
singing:

give me more of dis
feel good all day long

give me more of dis
what mamas keep from her daughters

who done gone from her breasts

Big Momma's Hands

Hands are roadmaps to lead and
follow to the next
her worn fingers have traced much
but she outlines my face, now
and I am new and water and birth and touch sweet milk
from Nefertiti's womb unattained in your life book she
has a degree in mama history and teaches me to count
blessings and the lucky star in my organic self when
she plates pancake prayers at the dining room table baby
sis blinks and drinks at mommy's breast as molasses
pour on top of maple soaked toast with fluffy center
preserved fresh from peach and strawberry orchard out
back yellow egg pillows sugar wheat porridge soft in
bowls
pig bacon burnt edges wrinkled crispy to perfection
a time to grab a hand and bow your head and be
thankful be grateful for this home heaven.

A Mother's Child

---

momma's love is a deep wide blanket
warm-forgiving with cream at her breasts
and, rich bronze skin kissed with sweat
cradled in navel nourish a cane-sugar
dipped-recipe
with heavy arms to handle me firmly

momma's flesh is tight. oil smooth.
stitched and wrapped me tightly in
tattered burlap satchel; a sea of
lemons and raining sun for deep
orange to kiss our lips.

gw'on chil gw'on

One Hand at a Time

---

a mellow silhouette lingers in dimmed noise.
Finger joints arthritic crooked and shake as eyes
focus hard in bifocal squinting. Sunrays strike
doormat in between the lampshade and blues.

    "Day break come late. Seem
only time it be's dat way
      wen huh triflin' selfs come roun' he'uh."

Nails curve in chipped burgundy paint
to snap close curtain blinds when
noon haze sets in. Brown coffee mug
sits on a nearby table, wrinkled letters
lay crumbled-scattered. Vehicle door in
the driveway slams
pulling the front door to the house open

    Oh, Lawdy. What has de devil done sent he'uh?

She ain't seen her in a month of Sundays but
that's her baby milk. Some seasons it's a
sour-bitter chosen too early spoiled at the
core, just rotten. Other times, it come
honeydew sugared.

    Good thang, she here now...

    "Don't forget bout' dat door, baby."

Struggling to keep the lawn cut grass smells outside.
And there she is.
Tight-smooth legs stand in narrow hallway across
heavy-thick varicose ones. Don't matter much
now
until silence sets in. Just the
breeze of a cracked-window
whistles the evenings chill in a
coded language.
It speaks. She smiles. Nice.
Bow-legged. Skin like buttermilk. Girl.
First reaction then and ain't nothin' changed.

> *Still got dem eyes, ocean set. Got Stanley*
> *written all o'vah dat chil,' don't chu know.*
> *Make a smile come o'vah me jus thankin' bout*
> *em.*

"Well come he'ah chil'. Let me get a
good look at chu.'"

Mens out here got eyes for this one.
Womanly juices shake from breasts,
hip bone, backside, thigh meat big-
boned and half-grown.

"Well, look at my baby. Don' come a long way!
Go put ya thangs down, got somethin'
hot on de stove..."

boney fingers woven in mine,
together. Since last, eyes done
caught some wave too distant to
calm.

"Now chil', now…"

Grasped my hand and cried.

"Don't got nobody."

Spoken softy. Softly told me,
one step at a time

Inspired by Reine

Proverbs 4:23

---

above all else, guard your heart,
for everything you do flows from it

familiar words read and spoken calloused hands palm
the bible that hold it an album of photos, hair,
obituaries, history, letters all in one book and as i
touch the inserted pages i unravel to become the
little girl who still lives in me and has learned that
life can be painful and lonely with an impending
sense of loss i know this feeling too well

      spanish moss point me to
colorful meals and brown people
all shades of summer

      mama's mother
      was soul food in the kitchen
that's where it went down
      hand-washed pork-rind bacon
catfish
      shrimp and peppers
fried chicken
      getting togethers

      mama
      the queen of it all

the house filled with people packed-in
all cousins aunties, siblings, uncles
it's a sunday for brass horns after the
gospel and prayers of course

grandmother
sits in her house chair
daddy's mama with darkness and
strength in her skin perseverance all
dreaming under a midnight sky

silent vibrations skip in her chest cavity blur tears
and hold uncertainty i build a metal wall and security
door for protection both old and new can feel the
familiar and comfortable   all inherited and learned by
women
and the stories they tell
heartbreak syndrome is a
scar you can't see
always been that way

to bury, push aside, keep going my mom was that
woman who everyone said you need to leave him
"you have a daughter and she needs you"

all three mothers will be leaving soon to
await the arrival of an unknown guest
since we've become a family torn and
breaking slowly from one funeral to
the next

a child can sing the beat of a mother's love
closest thing to her, at one time or the other but

we are finding ways to mend a broken heart
and i am learning new ways
to love myself
today tomorrow
hereafter

In Memory of Great Uncle Irvine (Jerome) Hunter

One Lesson to the Next

there are generations that have come and gone...
all rooted from the same tree

he was born into this world named
by one of sixteen girls
six children third in line soon before
other siblings much later

branched from southern warm roots
traditional family gatherings the
usual- wide-eared porch talks jive
talking card games the newest
dance moves- Charleston, mashed
potato all wrapped in mama's arms
in Motown tunes

shirts pattern- patched hand-stitch
britches on school nights after
dinner plates acting a fool with
little sister

out of his siblings he was the one who made women's
heavy legs crossed in musical heals made wide legged
men with seasick waves greased and parted
hold their stomachs teary eyes

46

in unrestrained deep gutted
knee slapping laughing
fits
we a part of it all

found solace in actions unspoken of not often the best
choice but never meant to be that way either so to be
there meant he couldn't be here to exist here meant he
sometimes couldn't be near and though that's a turmoil
we all have felt at some point in time he was proud of
his children and he honored his family

his life teaches us that good men are human too and
yeah they make mistakes, from time to time but we live,
we learn, pick up the pieces scrambled together for
sense making
we move forward
and won't forget

beloved son brother
nephew cousin
father grandfather
great grandfather
uncle, great uncle
yes, you will be
missed cherished
remembered

and don't you forget
there were troubles there
were victories there were
silent moments loud
memories and lessons to
be learned:

*everything is everything don't let
nobody steal your joy try the best
you can don't let no one rain on
your parade same song different
dance a house is an empty building
a home is where love stands you
don't destroy what you love
be grateful for God's hands*

all words left and, if you have the memory to
gather the sounds to sit planted among us life
and legacy of a tree that keeps growing yes it
does keeps sowing seeds in-numerically
numbered
to leave a message to teach

in every generation that sits in your very seat
we honor you, we thank you because
we too are all branches from the
same rooted tree

As told and inspired by my mama, Le'Donna

a call on monday morning

God woke me up this morning
told me to ask you something

What are you reaching for?

Tomorrow isn't promised
but death is
guaranteed.

Find the beauty in struggle and pain,
it could have happened to anybody but
it happened to you.

Baby, when things are going wrong all
around you, it's not the person, it's the
thing. The devil believes in God he was
God's favorite angel. Fight that spirit
rebuke its name and you claim the victory.
There is beauty in the thorn of a rose. That same
thorn went into the forehead of a man named Jesus
hung his head and rose on that mountain in Calvary.

I don't mean to bother you, take
you away from your day but God
told me to check on you, this
early Monday morning.
The same thing that tempted our ancestors
will be there for you too. You have to be

strong in God and stay encouraged.
Don't take people for granted
I know too well of what it feels like to
have people be taken away, that kind of
pain stays with you.

Know your heart and slow down.
Don't forget that the things that
you are running to, are only
temporary. Take time to smell
look feel.
Appreciate your life give
God your time humble
yourself.

Be in love own your passion release
and forgive you are of love you are
made from love you are a miracle
listen to God when he's talking to you
God has a powerful plan for your life

I'm just telling you
HE had me to call you

to deliver this
message
on this early Monday morning

Now, if anything ever happens to me
you better remember everything I'm telling you-

    I will.

Beyond the Sycamores

AUTUMN

PART ONE

Candlelit Lanterns

To the unseen wings

that pat the sky at night,

I am to be greeted

warmly

In the Meantime

i will know you in the meantime bread
dough stale with wrapping napkins when i
watch them all wrapped up in body
luggage and hanging still near the ceiling,
i am afraid. each pinned eyelid rotate
faces shatter beautifully on the living floor
nailed into cement

them is what i be like

sought vision to come on haunting me in
the silver of silence, i drape them with
belonging when wooden door waits with
sound bites
a fragmented warmth, growing

they say, the
old woman,
rooted and
branched
inside panel
73' since the citizen's battle each
tide rocking in an eight-year
premonition

the day end rainfall resume to
awaken the earth each hallway
gone children walked before there.
each one cry at night.

but no one believes

it is morning come with blue Sadie and
butter grits. a gentle brown, waving over
buggy straw but the woman
still breathing in the walls are kinks of
memories left in raw to glide down
paper shred when fists bring the scent
back kneaded thick and heavy down
yonder.
surface pines boiled in
sweet basket water each
drop of God's cry
is mine and yours

Candlelight

they were different. hands.
eyes. feet.
everything different.
said,

love never came

but
it
burns
strong
all the
same.

tribal markings were hieroglyphics
draped across your homeless back but
it burned strong all the same.
tears tumble down hilly cheeks when doors open and
shut each face, fragmented and strange hanging on
the other side of flesh covered walls i, too, am a
stranger-neighbor visiting for years to come.
forbidden to the symmetry of my beating skin
asleep to the screaming sirens of the world

body was stiff, moist and cold.
i am hurting for you to make
summer babies under our
moon
but

i am a black tunnel and
you no longer belong.

something was taken from me.
but you said,

it's cool.

unravel each knot between my thighs.
slip into each protected line until you
would disappear every piece of your face-
fabric unraveling, a rippling-ribbon in the
winds bellowing passed city window
riding buses and trains always again.

it is getting dark, now. and i must take the pastel
blues and pinks of each sky-painting with me.
out of this empty space where we once belonged.
i must return it
all of it

even you

Leaving Him

I can't hold you in my arms no more
    you bring the sun to my eyes warmth to my
    door

I can't keep you here can't
    keep you near

you said you never felt strength like
    this chick over here

you left your watch and tie and everything
    between

I never thought you could be so
    damn mean

you tell me you never felt a
    love like this before

you bring heart to my breasts, and
    soul to my hips

you bring the hum to a bird, and
    sugar to my lips

I can't believe
    I held on so long like this

Magic

---

shard glass is open scars that obliterate my duplicity
i am on a roof top laughing my heart to shreds
when moon does his little dance at dusk shattering
the sky into jumbled, mirrored pieces.
he leaves me feeling musk all over myself
but i'll have it no other way you are patience,
like i said. never could take it back from me.
but i repose.

your arms are holding me your arms braided long
across buxom and pressed breasts tight ear-face
joints.
i am a torn basket of sorted lemons
all ripe and shiny on a high shelf
moist and pregnant at the core
with green earth pushed in jars. i'll
have it no other way.

Remembering July

The sky was a blanket of fireflies
a quiet gathering of tiny lamps holding up the sky arm
was God. Hope my prayers are silent
and heard.
I, too, am here.
My ear, a window, all wrapped and holding still.
I'm sorry that I can't clean out your luggage bag
mine still has a full belly without fingers. It's
tied with pregnant raspberry leaves when my
hands are interlocked in yours,
the moon hangs swinging dripping over my
shoulder bones for magenta blues against
the eclipsing sun.

Belong to Me

In this midnight dance, heat rests on my fingertips when I touch you ever so gently one push and my soul is flying out cars and planes and homes I am with you again. you and I, ahold of each keep us hungry for more of this rush when we cry together to make life breathe into this child that will soon arrive body and soul rocking you had me walking on rose petal cushions my swollen belly in your working limbs this tied and protected womb child love shakes the earth when you move inside me teaching me how potted plants wait for hands to come to massage its soul to sleep

Sacred

---

on this sacred day i come before you my
soul all wrapped up into the warm
embrace of a man's protection strong &
proud of a woman's bosom beautiful &
glorious

they say, *when an*
elder speaks bring
your ear close
to the drumbeat

you are the man my father prayed for
faith unwavering for his youngest child
but it was your smile & voice the
hands of a warrior the heart of a
champ
that brought us to this very place

you are the dream that God sent to me
at the genesis of our existence tongue;
gentle, honest, forgiving eyes;
caring, humble, earnest

you done seen many things yes,
you have

& this love burns strong
all the same past

this love is one that I have prayed for

& i can tell you we will see rainy
days & sunny rays we will endure
& withstand it all
because you you were born
for me as adam to eve from
the rib bone like sand-lines &
moonstones
rocking in an ocean of raindrops

where the origin of our legacy begins
born to bare seed with you for a
harvest of values to raise a family
positioned before all who love us;
seen us grow
been there many moons

but where does the story end? you
ask.

love never ends
it only knows
beginnings

i will

---

let it come to my feet
i will cherish you
      let it motion a hand
i will walk with you let it
whisper into my ear i will understand
you   let it tickle the nape of my
neck
      i will surrender to you let it come
with a kiss i will reminisce about you
let it touch, the tender of my torso
      i don't remind you
let it catch the texture of my tresses
i have to find you   let it come
in a bottle
      i will send for you let
it show me love

      i will
      fall
      with you

PART TWO

It Don't *S h i n e* Like It Used To

*Mamas
dont pray
over dem kind of
names*

welfare ballad

---

      ya got a baybe
well tell me sumthin
      ya got a baybe

in the morning got
the food stamps
baby tell me
sumthin don't be
mean got the milk
baybee
i tell ya, life aint free

i keep um coming, like the noon days
keeps it hot on the porch on the sun days
got the butter with the corn bread see
the mother she make the cream and cool
spread
tell ya sumthin
dont be mean got
the chittlins got
the cabbage
and the pig feet

into the night i got the
stomach soul i keeps
the hungry fed i keeps
um feelin so

tell ya sumthin

aint, nothing like that summer breeze
tell ya sumthin aint, nothing like
that sugar tea tell ya sumthin aint
nothing like that bit of cheese tell
ya sumthin
aint nothing like that baybe

ya got a baybe
       well tell me sumthin
ya got a baybe
       give me some uh dat summer

   free

mademoiselle ebony

she is dead. & it is dawn when she awakens in the
silentlonely house each limb pulling her from heavens
deep orange shade quilted shield & sugar pies across the
termite eaten floor boards
she sits elegantly to meet her reflection
she sits until her sky rage black & blue
creole tresses, thrown onto high and
sharp shoulders cutting with each
search of an embryo-splitting womb
a rising fire near her rib cage

sunrise to dusk makes her womanly scent change
a statue in bones & skin & flesh still
in the rough and murky marsh
floating in
cascading waves

Bystanders
___

Nearby people wave at my porch steps I am but a
woman with silence in her ear I can hear the way
your lips form curses gifted at my doorstep curses
flick with tongues when lights close in my face
an eraser of cascading mountains left virgin-like

the arms of moss cover my house like wind storms
inside, the earth is planted and potted dense in heavens
deep orange shade of morning weaves a new batch for
the innards some people's souls left tangled in empty
preserves by magnolia's that tip their flowers to old
ladies on Sundays like the others

I will be remembered
for some time

the jungle

---

we all speak the same. got
the same dreams.
consume the same things.
we the same out here.

flies and baby bother me on my way to
salt sugar rush wise street talkers offer
their sense "the know-how" manual.

washed-up
beat-on
women
flap their lips to teach me

        they aint me

we all survive
    righteously
unforgivingly

pull the sling-shot screen back walk
into my square
bills due
dishes piled up in warm oily hair strand water
roaches crawl scatter on counter pot scrapings
stacked way to high on innocent eyes that sweaty
man spits venom down my neck that chill and protect
me

        where
my change
you,
           b-?
fist
force
jaw
ajar
in
crimson loss mama
say

      change never comes when you waits for it

    i ain't always been like this

      was one of them pretty girls
          you can't forget

his hands are blunt-stained finger-webs that
pry my baby boy's eyes wide
to watch his sins
      a child's love never dies

noon air cool the needle burn in
my skin down blood and cry
run dry lines to cheek and chin

it's been morning for quite some time

two years but still

sun don't shine on west project
like it used to

Mama Works

To me, mama came, heels work her heels when men work her mind. Tears fell from her eyes, between each cry, an unheard lie was the demise. Printed letters with blue ink spreading tired names and games across the page was his rage. Too much, got too many of them ways that could make a man-he wants-to-play, but at the same time, wipe the sadness off mama's face. He wants to show her, but now all he can do is pace. All she can do is taste what was left without him, four years, now in his place. Still in the race, though he moves like Oshun. He plans to make his way, but her actions explain that, no, he can't stay. No longer is this your space by the moon.

This woman, this strong woman, to keep her man, she prays. By her nightstand she sway's, feelings built into the rays. No longer does she feel the days that stripe her bed covers is where she stays. "Can't feel a thang," is what she say cause she longs for this man to bring back her back-bone ways. From her, mother lies. Although, pride denies it. Mother is blind. Mama watches the turquoise skies when it rains. Pain running like paint-like stains that keep her face looking sane during lunch hours where long white legs stand. Beautiful and straight. But mama's mind can sense the fate. Walking into the front door. He just took off his shoes sore. He makes one move more before bringing his body past the door. Bringing the energy and the cologne that rides every mood like salt on mama's sores.

This is what this man brings. He works her mind after hours, nonsense on his breath when he whispers she whimpers and I can't help but to hold my temper because this woman I call mama, she has really left. This man of theft takes mama's strength leaving her limber, leaving her worn and dry as timber. I want her to open her eyes. I want her to remember. How life would come to her eyes before she would smile then cry. Told me how she and her mama went to the sun to fly. Tales told about some men who made laughter spread into their thighs after they pocketed the change. It made them all the same. All like names. Plenty. Like mama, there are plenty. Much to change, there is much to change. This is the man that rides her mind. That keeps her from promise, keeps her in lies. Keeps her from home, keeps her from time. This is a mother who don't shine no more. She don't smell like pine no more. She ain't mine no more.

She's Baby Mines

Brown Baby was a ball of silk, resting in the knot of my palm with the finest dark curls and a pair of almonds for eyes- smoky gray color.
They told me,

He gon' be special.

But you were already special,
since the
beginning.

You rested in the lining of my tired eyes, held you inside the color much different from the new gray knowing, it would someday change
but the eyes lost its density much
sooner than later.
Now, they wonder why she called some devil,
love.
When
since the beginning, both devil and
love put together had took on a whole
other meaning floating in a twenty-one-
year revelation.
came kicking and screaming something terrible
and   you,   you   were hardly even
there.

mama say,

stay wetter in the wash-bin.

But
my tides
have
already come

Inside Home Pt. 1

My daddy and my father My
daddy and my father My
daddy and my father My
daddy and my father
Now

Patience sizzles cake muffins on the stove top
sweet to the eye inside, when walked into my inside
burning bright reds knew you wouldn't burn me
though you watched me move about the kitchen.
Nothing more or less pushing less than two doll
babies and "more than life at your feet" told me
that.
Listened, me.
As I creased the morning tile lines in
a hop scotch you never knew.
Heard mama say you knew the scotch very well, though.
In a pan on the stove once where sugar set in. But
something changed when you loosened your grip on the
pan-handle, wrapped yellow tight fists in choke hold.
Mama inside arms.
Baby outside arms.
And red stillness red
stillness on
yellow flesh

My daddy and my father My
daddy and my father My
daddy and my father My
daddy and my father Now

75

"apple in my eye mama" but you never heard me in them woods.
White plank in the middle with people.
And "probably mimicking some pet name my peoples done gave her.
Laughter in her haunted baby belly.
So young.
Blew me a kiss in a smile.
Lips tight and lined.
A drop of sweat rests on the slip of your chin.
But have to keep moving keep moving.
Your fingers encircle atop some woman's spinning head as sweat kicked from earth to your stomach. That night

My daddy and my father My
daddy and my father My
daddy and my father My
daddy and my father
Now

Working eyes where loosen sockets next to the kitchen counter. The tears that never came sat dormant in mine. Hidden somewhere past some place we once called "home" on a street where the fire began
inside arms.
Outside in the nights burning air.
Two long pigtails and a bright orbit behind me Where your great mama's words were all but said, "nevah look back baby." all she said.
Lit me straight to her room door, cracked open with flickering light and muffled tones. When I found something so strong so weak. Crawled in strong arms, head resting on the heaving bosom.

So strong how she wide tooth combed the tresses wavy
and stroked the cheek in a cotton dress. Face lines
woven beside the wrist in threads. Woven spiced and
sweet on those nights.

My daddy and my father My
daddy and my father My
daddy and my father My
daddy and my father
Now

Gliding from the house under
the doors
swarming the streets like scattered, black marbles "they
sho' nuff' lucky," you could hear them. Spit between
the black pit in their teeth.
But we would have never known.
Left a scratch on the memory and can't ever let it go.
How their house became our home.
I asked him,
"so, daddy- where is our home?" when
he looked inside.

My daddy and my father My
daddy and my father My
daddy and my father My
daddy and my father
Now

"well, it gets a little complicated
when you lookin' to get an answer
from a tight squeeze, but-" Nine
months to reflect what was crimson
by the kitchen sink.

Heavy eyelids in a new yellow.
And the room- is heavy. So heavy.
When the baby cries the first time and
the eyes are yellow.

My daddy and my father My
daddy and my father My
daddy and my father My
daddy and my father
Now

"sweat and tears is in this pot," called a "storm" cause
don't know it's coming. when it do it's neither spiced or
sweet. you pick to choose."

When the scent thickens and linger from great mama's
tender neck skin to fruit. A smile on a string of strength.
 So when these hollow lives ask me about this "storm,"
I give them a long winded,
"no. I will leave it to mama to explain."
We fled on mama's tears that night.
All three lives. One inside arms. And
the other, in hand.
"nevah look back baby" was all she said.

My daddy and my father My
daddy and my father My
daddy and my father My
daddy and my father My
daddy and my father My
daddy and my father

Now

sirens

---

sirens are church bells too distant to feel keep
us breathing and grieving
for hot heat street
fever meter

got a hold on us   all
us waiting to take
away
always take away

dont know what flesh blood on concrete smell like, do
you? it scream it laugh it sing and never die

dead body too heavy to carry. it fall
everywheres and dont wake up it
piss on itself like a drunk fool
it wait for momma

        drag it off the street
        from under the yellow car lamp

        aint no momma
aint nobody out here

but us

whatever you do with that body
that drumbeat dont move

it still gonna be there

it still gonna be there
no matter how long your cries turn to sleep

it still gonna be there no
matter
how skin-sticky peel back on bed sheet

it still gonna be there

no matter
how
      long

you hum
that child soul
to dream

  just waiting to take away

  always take away

A Mother's Tears

my child has a story, too

there was poison in the roots long before the night you
were born centuries back invisible people chose your
skin not to love you were born with a veil second
sight, conjurer child the day i laid eyes on you tried to
keep you safe but i had demons of my own to
surrender to
gift of prophesy tells me death is on your face it is
a virus that lies dormant with any word-lesson
spoken is not enough to save him he must learn-on-
his-own he is my son and the killer of your daughter
your child was taken from you mine has long since
been gone our roots are from a distant land the origin
of its conception is complex been transplanted, and
since, fighting to survive because momma wasn't
there to rest your head, make sure all was well daddy
wasn't there to prepare your prayers against the world
from empty mouth in famished food desert
toxic wastewater to resuscitate the body
unemployable welfare dependent subsistence
miseducation- pathway to confinement mass
incarceration- new age slavery
the virus is both traveling and in remission
from birth-school neighborhood-church to
funeral-court prison-grave
people lose their lives in this human kind of war too
many dead men walking and i see them i know their
names

haunts me like no other i have met your
child who visits my home in the
midnight hour speaks to me
tells me i am the lifeline of her killer that her death
began with me as her mother i can only whisper
when i tell her… violence is a disease, cyclical
generational systemic curse yet curable- a deep
emotional scar penetration uncover it, peel back the
wound lacerate bacteria before spread through
branch-limb, trunk-bone can't have another yet be
named dead on these streets i stand on sacred ground
when i tell you at the crossroads of incarceration and
liberation the child on that screen connected to a
murder scene to confess sins and magnified flaws
aint mine- that is not the child i raised i tried my
best, Lord knows i did all i could to protect him
but it just wasn't enough and i
couldn't do it all by myself
the death of your child is
the imprisonment of mine
053299 to replace a consecrated blessed reputation
my son was gonna be somebody
i had plans for my boy but *he has been dead a long time*
the world tells me before he found the gun the
remembered spirit tells me we have been here before
the darker race- brought for a silent- obedient
resurrection under the diagnosis of fear and terrorist to
inhabit rather than inherit the earth
truth of it all; it's in the roots you may need to dig
them up a bit veiny venomous roadmaps to the soul
confession of spiritual trauma endured for some time,
now
and hope is a purple that i ask for forgiving and
repented i hang my head let the tears unfold, collected

and swollen from tired-tight pressure pain can't be
shield from this bright light pointed at my color we both
are patients in this infirmary childless matriarchs and
have lost much beloved, I am sorry there is an untold
story that says loss is a barren tree without fruit and this
proverb needs unearthing to reconcile for what was
done cannot be undone. yet there remains an answer in
the thick of this numbness we search for ourselves in
this story is ours
and i pass it down to you to disrupt
this curse born in water and spirit
replacement of poison with promise
will take a village
in redemption, regeneration, restoration it
is the revelation
if it's in the roots, it's in the branches
now, healing
manifest with
mercy as remedy
and let be always
in love and memory

Inside Home Pt. 2

*my brother is my father my
brother is my father my
brother is my father my
brother is my father now*

blew me from his fist, but i never really knew its true meaning. my ear against the wall the air conditioner blows out words and dotted the heads in sheer, line bulbs. made them glow, oh, so pretty that it put a smile on my face. and baby, let me tell you, i ain't smiled since the woman melted into the kitchen flooring. from the burning all night! it shot from his nostrils. the growl of his bottom lip twisting his words. so twisted. and, "you know he wrung that woman to crumbles" but it's a different night for these women.
"so tragic. that woman must'a knew it was coming! she saw the reds didn't *she?*" *no-no.*
not at all.
and both women done jumped out their cushions, standing with bent knees, wide eyed
because like her,
they, too, see.

*my brother is my father my
brother is my father my
brother is my father my
brother is my father now*

    yeah, behind them is the arm meat and the sweating nose, made their heads round into the night the flames

hit her home four hours and twelve tears ago. one tear
for each year. after her baby baby belly sank- she cried
the rest of her life. what the colors did when the baby
loosened from this here woman- child's uterus.
"wasn't she given all dem awards at dat one place?" said
one.
"all 'at don't mattah right now" the other retorted.
kept her eyes on the memory and they saw it. they
were taken across the street. it was a yesterday. a
very close day, when the mouths dropped and the
smell of burnt rubber caught the eyelids stuck. *no-
no. this woman did not.* this woman is much too
beautiful *and* light to be the name fallen from *this*
story.
"honey, color never mattered at a time like this"—
"oh" at a time like
this?

my brother is my father my
brother is my father my
brother is my father my
brother is my father now

"baby, my daughter put a pistol to my son's head- at a
time like this." nothing but space set them apart, and
memory. the exact time when the scotch was strong. his
knuckles were too. *push* after throwing my son into the
ended bedroom air. she thought she threw something
into the bedroom.
no, it wasn't her son, her strength flew from her body
when she began to melt- into the bedroom. thought to
protect the son, but the yellows and reds soaked into the
tender pores when the mothers hairmouthfingerslegs
all began to melt together. i was there.

woman's daughter   *and,* the women can't
believe this here beautiful not to mention, light
skinneded girl was involved.

my brother is my father my
brother is my father my
brother is my father my
brother is my father now

when them women heard the final story, didn't know
"how the fire spread the way it did, though?" i never
really knew the yellows and the reds true meaning. but
it's in the history. i knows it. in the fire, before the
woman thought she was saving one person the second
had already been branded. the skin, a deep yellow and
red. it was red. the color beat that woman's insides into
the flooring until she melted in twelve tears and he
thought i was just going to watch? this is a love, i will
never forget. and memories in a three inch-toilet
cell- a body line zipped all the way up until it can't
breathe.
that
is all
that
i
want
to
know

my brother is my father my
brother is my father my
brother is my father my
brother is my father my

brother is my father my
brother is my father

now

Happily Ever After

Once upon a time, in a
faraway land a young
prince awaited his
father's strong hand.

There were days he felt unwanted
in the fatherless home for a
manly figure to rear him into
growth.

Because he was a prince, see, he
was thought not on his own but
what they ceased to notice the
figure missing by his throne.

There were months he held his mother
who used to mirror might with a scent
the cool of lavender a smile the
warmth of light.

His mother, hurting for many years
the pain is just too much single-
parent, three jobs six children,
metro on the bus.

The pain he knows his family holds
shoots through his skin and bone he
decides to make a choice
manifesting in his soul.

He prays, "Oh Lord, please
take my hand and guide
me through this struggle."
He continues, "I ask for
hope and faith,
GOD shield me from the rubble."

But loneliness brought the streets
and the streets brought the drugs.
A toxic lifestyle in your body is
stylish for a princely- thug.

For once, the boy thought he had it all
lavish, material things to see but, on
the inside was his greatest fight to
become the man to be.

Hopeless, woke him in the morning
anger, his sleepless night constant
drama from wrongdoings are
reminders things aren't right.

Wisdom says, "Don't give up the fight,
for you are not alone look to a higher
spirit to tread your footprints on the
road."

No longer is he prince, but a man
awaiting rein, to become the king his
father could have, if had not strayed
away.

This man, he fights adversity it's
time to make a change he walks

onto the college campus face,
clothes, hair-all look the same.

But difference is not appearance but
the work in him, God gave speak
life into conception and breath into
a phrase.

At sunrise he prays the prayer of Paul,
"Lord, I feel the wisdom of your spirit."
At sunset, the prayer of David,
"Thankful that, you God, have steered it."
Dawn, is the prayer of Jabez,
"I ask for one blessing, Father."
And Dusk, is the night of day,
that lifts all prayers higher.

You might recognize this man on
the surface, you would recall but
when he speaks, his head is high,
his posture, grand and tall.

Many thought he wouldn't survive he
would end up like the rest nameless
people envied his strength even when
he passed the test.

Today, this king is driven humble,
courageous, not to mention.
confident, loving, honest, man of
powerful conviction.

See, this king was once a man this
man was once a boy this boy was

once a prince if you know the
preface to this story.

No matter the conditions, teach
children limitless dreams family is
royal and sacred and was created for
kings and queens.

An Intricate Tapestry

WINTER

PART ONE

With G O D

*Be centered in the spirit world
honor what has come today and before*

*to reproduce new ripe fruit
& grow fertile again*

*what was
already been
there all along*

Dedicated to my father, Tyrone Clifford Wells

A Daughter's Prayer

I hold you in my dreams roots long and
swinging vines from heavenly seeds
shades of lilac under your smile it has
rained cause you've been gone for a
while for each mile and miles away
cause you've been gone just for a while.

The blues seep between your skin
pour from your skin my heart
cord pulls for you I hold you in
my dreams my soul pumps fuel
for two.

It has been many years July
shores sweep summer doors my
head is bowed my knees are
heavy I can only hum, "Dear
Lord."

I hold you in my dreams the
blues seep between my skin
it has been many years

since this quiet
pain, came
tumbling in.

Dedicated to: Great Aunt Susie Wells Duncan

A 101 Year Legacy

On the day you were born
the Lord kissed the earth opened the sky and
brought sunlight into the world

I thank God for this creation for
your life
I, too am from this legacy

spirit and flesh
patchwork-woven entangled
deeply rooted to birth something
new for this world to honor-
remember

you were brought into this world and given back to God
wrapped in your mother's warm arms your father
holding the Bible and reading from the book of Psalms
planting sugar kisses under your soft neck carefully
stroking the straight black hairs atop your head holding
gently a handful of blessings

you were a prayed for child
you and your siblings
were

soaking and manifesting in an orange-ripe sun shower to
sing colorfully beneath the lilac skyline
to dance carelessly under the sharp brightness of the
stars

to share stories under the moon's pull
to listen for thunder heavy call to hold
out palms to catch rain puddles as it
will remind you to

live in the moment
respect those who come first into this world live every
second like it's your last tomorrow is not promised
be grateful for all that you have and come to know
hope, and love, and struggle and victory and all that it
brings with it and over the seconds to minutes from
hours to days from weeks to months, from years to
decades every experience that once was and will be has
shaped the woman who stands before you, today

backbone strong-willed standing class and
elegance and beauty and intelligence
and just as new as the first day of birth

from soul southern summers and butter grits to
east mountain wind storms and porch chimes
from northern lake streams and Motown sounds
to where we stand today
right here in this space in time

your life tells me
what you stand for what
you dream for what you
give to this world
your contribution
is worth living for

memory
time
life
people

is all we have in this world
to be remembered by

it is the number of times
we serve and give and
teach and forgive and
learn and reach
the time that we share and serve

so thank you for the early days and late years thank you
for all the words that you continue to speak thank you
for the long strides that you courageously take
thank you for the strength that your heart will keep but
most importantly thank you for giving us a legacy
for all of us to
follow and lead

Sap and Leaves

I am from native patchwork
from mason jars and honey pots
I am from the brick homes of heavy-armed women and
strong-backed men, brown-brave it smelled like
Saturday morning perm burning some woman's scalp
fried chicken popping in the iron grease skillet all on the
same schedule
I am from the natural Mahogany roots growing in the
circle where God and human hands meet in glory
I am from the VHS recorded visits to Grandma's house
and high cheekbones and big legs from Annie Campbell
Wells and Roberta Chatman Morris and Ulah Mae
Means

I am from the funny bone that laughs all night, plays
cards, tells jokes, and pops fingers while singing
Motown till the midnight sky bleeds blue ink hours into
a sun spotted rose morning and where every sibling
shared the same worn bed and warm pissy sheets
from "there is a secret land behind that small closet
door" and "you are the most precious child in this
here world." I am from redgreenblue puddles of
paint-stained glass window church on Sundays
where heads wrapped and shoulders dip in blessed
waters from deep tear-filled eyes where gifted
premonitions are told in the hold of someone's
palms

I am from Pensacola, Detroit, Pembroke, Madison
County, Little Rock,
New Orleans, and Louisville hot water cornbread,
seafood gumbo, white-bass fish, black-eyed peas,

coconut lemon butter pound cake, and room
temperature water from an African woman who bore
16 girls by a white plantation owner the classy and
poised Creole woman who held power in her bosom
and secrets in her recipe inside a photo album- sticky
film pressed folded and overflowing under some aunty
cousins living room coffee table

I am from flowered wallpaper plastic covered furniture
hardwood floors and carpeted staircases where
country and city meet with open arms and where doors
never close

SHE: A ballad for sistah

Sistah Sistah, hear me now you
are strong and you are proud
leadership is in your soul
manifest and you will grow.

Sistah Sistah, speak your mind,
have courage to define the
resilience in your lungs
re-write the lyrics that are sung.

Sistah Sistah, there were trials that
tried to kick you to the ground. Didn't
know if you'd withstand. It took
persistence to get out, but you made it,
you got through to help women just
like you:

*She can't help to rub her agitated hands because
it's now that she can't believe it.*

*She turned to the nurse practitioner and
said, "Right now, is not the season. A
season accruing warmth, laughter, youth
not to mention pleasing."*

*See, it made her mind reason, because in
her heart, she thinks she needs it.*

*She's holding past the cotton shirt that
denies her body eating.*

*Alone, but holding on, she
takes the book and she's
starting to read it.*

*Mapped into the pages
are their eyes their
lungs are pleading.*

*She reaches to touch their face
because like them she can't
stop breathing.*

Sistah Sistah, self-esteems assurance
that personifies endurance, have
confidence and persevere allow God
to reassure you.

Sistah Sistah, the epitome of fortitude
passion and hope are key. Oh ye of
little faith, it only takes a mustard
seed. Always keep hope and elevate
your abilities.

Sistah Sistah, you are reaching past
the goals that you have set, you
have gone through many things, but
never do you forget, the stories, the
seasons the battles and the blessings
it was scarring and traumatic but it
was only a lesson.

Sistah Sistah, expect sunny skies and storms
throughout your life course if you swim
right through the tides you'll walk right off
the shore.

Sistah Sistah, restate your name reclaim
the spirit in your reign.
You are a Queen. You were chosen.
You are anointed and ordained.

Sistah Sistah, who are you?
Divine completion in full bloom.
Africa is the tree
while America is the fruit.

Sistah Sistah, I am you
I am the stride inside your move.
I am a woman who's renowned,
listen, this is what I've found-
claim your victory claim it now
fit the description wear the
crown.

Behind my Skin

twelve years ago today

from the city bus window in a midnight hour my hopes and dreams and plans are all growing inside of me

i am pregnant. i hide things under my skin. embryo kicks my eyes open. fetus hiccups during math tests. lecture class about my plans. to tell my story. but i am embarrassed. shame grips my baby waist. this child is innocent. from the things that makes me human. child dont deserve to repent. baby fingers and toes press and push against the silent earth inside me. for loud noise i cant hear yet. is a long revealing lesson i must soon face.

this one gon be tough, they say.

i clutch this child in my womb. want her
to see the mother she belongs to. carried
her nine months warm breathing.
held her four days cold breathless it's the birthday of
another child somewhere in the world
breasts throb full and pull from a body that wasn't
prepared to be a mother just so soon heart pours from
new and unfamiliar vacant pores that ache slowly but i
must smile, hug and thank the people who brought
flowers to the funeral and filled the water pitcher.

and prepare for all that lies ahead of me all that i
am and to become
woman. wife. mother. daughter. sister. artist. writer.
student. doctor. teacher but at the end of the day i
am all that the earth will have me to be.

so, ten years ago, today

i'd tell that girl whose face sits illuminated
in the city bus window whose hopes and dreams
and plans are all growing inside of her
don't you dare give up now

it's gon be tough

but

so are you

Just Become

when you couldn't stand no
longer could you stand you
purged that song from the fire
in your belly to release that
urge hold on to your dreams
touch its tears touch its fears
touch everything that makes
it holy and profane, and you
sing its heart to rest sing its
heart to rest

rock in its rumble reap in its ray hold onto it and
become unto it give reverence and speak it out and
let it out let it fumble for these letters and notes that
keep your soul abreast

reach out for that mountain and you
better climb each stone shed and reveal
to each earthbound trial you ain't done
yet you ain't done yet
live and lift with each tremble

with every limber thought that you could give to your
dreams, and you become
you become reverently
honesty integrity

just become

Healing

My daughter, Nadia Michelle Robinson's name means *Hope with God*. And she is my angel. At 17 years old, I carried my daughter for nine months during which I experienced for the first time, a life growing inside of me. However, with all the plans that I had to become a mother, I could not stop what God had already planned and ordained in my life.

When the doctors could not find a heartbeat using two different monitors, the reality that my daughter was gone began to flood my eyes. I had lived for this child and now she was gone, that fast. I had so many questions and wanted answers from the doctors but there were none. She was completely healthy.

So, after taking a pregnancy test, hiding my pregnancy from family, celebrating with three baby showers, sharing my plans as a future mother, and enduring judgmental stares, the news that my baby was "deceased" was devastating, heartbreaking, and traumatizing. It taught me a multitude of lessons with one being God is in control and has the final say.

Nadia gave me a larger purpose in life. She gave me a mother's heart and taught me the true meaning of resilience, hope, faith, determination, and perseverance. These values allowed me to survive a domestic violence relationship shortly after her death. Nadia empowered me to focus more on the gifts that God planted in me to share the insurmountable love that I have for my daughter with other children and families.

Although I did not understand God's plan for my life at the time, I am thankful for HIS grace and mercy. It has been twelve years since I lost my daughter, and I am still learning to heal. As you read this book, I hope and pray that it is a source of healing for you as you continue along your life's journey.

Walking to remember 10-15-07

Last year over 28,000 babies in United States were delivered dead. That rate is approximately one every 20 minutes.

Gov. Ernie Fletcher declared October as Pregnancy and Infant Loss Awareness Month in Kentucky, and in response a Walk to Remember was held earlier this month on Louisville's Great Lawn in remembrance of children lost to stillbirths, miscarriages and Sudden Infant Death Syndrome.

Tytianna Wells
University of Louisville

People discussed their experiences. One discussion was about stillbirths. Stillbirths are completely random and occur in about one in 200 pregnancies. Up to half of stillbirths occur during pregnancies that seem problem-free. While 14 percent of fetal deaths occur during labor and delivery, 86 percent occur before labor begins. ...

Anyone can lose a child. It seems like just yesterday when I learned that I was about to become a mother for the first time.

I never thought the first time would become a nightmare. I was a senior at one of the most prestigious educational institutions in Kentucky, and I remember the morning that I walked across the wide-rimmed stage of a vast auditorium and was handed my diploma. I lifted my eyes to the upper reaches where my family was seated and holding the pink teddy bear that I bought for my daughter's newly decorated room. ...

The bear was the last "something" that I had of her. Where had the oxygen exhaled from her lungs escaped to, I wondered. I dared not question with my lips; my eyes did the job for me when I cradled what little I had left to hold in my empty arms after nine months of her surviving in my womb. All that's left of her is the memory — the memory of my daughter rocking in the breeze of a silent death called stillbirth.

Manifesting

You have a story to tell. Allow this book to remind you of your life. Your story is your testimony and ministry. It has the power to heal. Use this space to reflect on your life experience and journey. Release what has been holding you back from accomplishing your dreams and achieving your life's purpose. Your story needs to be told.

1. *What is your story?*
2. *What accomplishments are you most proud of?*
3. *What disappointments have you faced?*
4. *What are you most passionate about?*
5. *What is holding you back from moving to the next level in your journey?*
6. *What sacrifices must you make to achieve your innermost potential, passion, and purpose?*
7. *What message will your legacy leave?*

ABOUT THE AUTHOR

Dr. Tytianna Nikia Maria Ringstaff was born in Detroit, Michigan, and raised in Louisville, Kentucky. As early as 5 years old, she was a budding storyteller, writer, and artist. As a graduate of the University of Louisville, she holds a dual Bachelor of Arts degree in English and Pan-African Studies (2009), a Master of Arts degree in Pan-African Studies (2012), and a Ph.D. in Curriculum and Instruction (2021). As CEO and founder of Honey Tree Publishing, Dr. Ringstaff is the author and illustrator of more than eight books. She has taught and performed internationally as an educator, artist, and activist. She lives in Louisville, Kentucky with her loving husband, Christopher, and family.

www.ingramcontent.com/pod-product-compliance
Lightning Source LLC
Chambersburg PA
CBHW030529010526
44110CB00048B/948